SAINT MONICA

"My brethren, if any of you err from the truth, and one convert him: He must know that he who causeth a sinner to be converted from the error of his way, shall save his soul from death, and shall cover a multitude of sins."

—James 5:19-20

Sotomajor

Vision at Ostia

SAINT MONICA

c. 332-387

MODEL OF CHRISTIAN MOTHERS

By

F. A. Forbes

"Who shall find a valiant woman? Far and from the uttermost coasts is the price of her. The heart of her husband trusteth in her, and he shall have no need of spoils. She will render him good, and not evil, all the days of her life...Her children rose up, and called her blessed: her husband, and he praised her."
—Proverbs 31:10-12, 28

TAN BOOKS AND PUBLISHERS, INC.
Rockford, Illinois 61105

Nihil Obstat: Edward Myers
            Censor Deputatus

Imprimatur: Edmund Canon Surmont
            Vicar General
            Westminster
            June 15, 1915

Originally published in 1915 by R. & T. Washbourne Limited, London, and B. Herder, St. Louis, Missouri, as *The Life of Saint Monica* in the series *Standard-bearers of the Faith: A Series of Lives of the Saints for Young and Old*, with three original illustrations by Frank Ross Maguire.

ISBN 0-89555-618-9

Library of Congress Catalog Card No.: 98-60284

Cover illustration: "Vision at Ostia," by Sotomajor. Photo courtesy of Augustinian Press, Villanova, PA.

Printed and bound in the United States of America.

TAN BOOKS AND PUBLISHERS, INC.
P.O. Box 424
Rockford, Illinois 61105
1998

"Bury my body anywhere; it does not matter. Do not let that disturb you. This only I ask—that you remember me at the altar of God wherever you may be."

—St. Monica to her sons
as she lay dying
far from home.

CONTENTS

This book is above all things the story of a mother. But it is also the story of a noble woman—a woman who was truly great, for the reason that she never sought to be so. Because she understood the sphere in which a woman's work in the world must usually lie and led her life truly along the lines that God had laid down for her; because she suffered bravely, forgot herself for others and remained faithful to her noble ideals, she ruled as a queen among those with whom her life was cast. Her influence was great and far-reaching, but she herself was the last to suspect it, the last to desire it, and that was perhaps the secret of its greatness. The type is rare at the present day, but, thank God! there are still Monicas in the world. If there were more, the world would be a better place.

SAINT MONICA

"Favour is deceitful, and beauty is vain: the woman that feareth the Lord, she shall be praised. Give her of the fruit of her hands: and let her works praise her in the gates."

—Proverbs 31:30-31

Chapter 1

A YOUNG CHRISTIAN GIRL

ON the sunny northern coast of Africa, in the country which we now call Algeria stood, in the early days of Christianity, a city called Tagaste. Not far distant lay the field of Zama, where the glory of Hannibal had perished forever. But Rome had long since avenged the sufferings of her bitter struggle with Carthage. It was the ambition of Roman Africa, as the new colony had been called by its conquerors, to be, if possible, more Roman than Rome. Every town had its baths, its theatre, its circus, its temples, its aqueducts. It was even forbidden to exiles as a place of refuge—too much like home, said the authorities.

It was about the middle of the fourth century. The Church was coming forth from her long imprisonment into the light of day. The successor of Constantine, in name a Christian, sat on the imperial throne. The old struggle with paganism, which had lasted for four hundred years, was nearly at an end, but new dangers

1

assailed the Christian world. Men had found that it was easier to twist the truth than to deny it, and heresy and schism were abroad.

In the atrium or outer court of a villa on the outskirts of Tagaste an old woman and a young girl sat together looking out into the dark shadows of the evening, for the hot African sun had sunk not long since behind the Numidian Mountains, and the day had gone out like a lamp.

"And the holy Bishop Cyprian?" asked the girl.

"They sent him into exile," said the old woman, "for his father had been a Senator and his family was well known and powerful. At that time they dared not put him to death, though later he, too, shed his blood for Christ. It was God's will that he should remain for many years to strengthen his flock in the trial."

"Did you ever see him, Grandmother?" asked the girl.

"No," said the old woman, "it was before my time, but my mother knew him well. It was when he was a boy in Carthage and still a pagan that the holy martyrs Perpetua and Felicitas suffered with their companions. It was not till years after that he became a Christian, but it may have been their death that sowed the first seed in his heart."

"Tell me," said the girl softly. It was an oft-

told tale of which she never tired. Her grandmother had lived through those dark days of
persecution, and it was the delight of Monica's
girlhood to hear her tell the stories of those who
had borne witness to the Faith in their own land
of Africa.

"Perpetua was not much older than you," said
the old woman. "She was of noble race and born
of a Christian mother, though her father was a
pagan. She was married and had a little infant
of a few months old. When she was called before
the tribunal of Hilarion the Roman Governor,
all were touched by her youth and beauty. 'Sacrifice to the gods,' they said, 'and you shall go
free.' 'I am a Christian,' she answered, and nothing more would she say, press her as they might.

"Her old father hastened to her side with the
baby, and laid it in her arms. 'Will you leave
your infant motherless?' he asked, 'and bring
your old father's hairs in sorrow to the grave?'

" 'Have pity on the child!' cried the bystanders.
'Have pity on your father!'

"Perpetua clasped her baby to her breast and
her eyes filled with tears. They thought she had
yielded, and brought her the incense.

" 'Just one little grain on the brazier,' they
said, 'and you are free—for the child's sake and
your old father's.'

"She pushed it from her. 'I am a Christian,'

she said. 'God will keep my child.'

"She was condemned with her companions to be thrown to the wild beasts in the amphitheatre, and they were taken away and cast into a dark dungeon. Every day they were tempted with promises of freedom to renounce the Truth. The little babe of Felicitas was born in the prison where they lay awaiting death. A Christian woman took the infant to bring it up in the Faith. The young mother never saw the face of her child in this world. One word, one little motion of the hand, and they would be free, restored again to their happy life of old and the homes that were so dear. There were many, alas! in those cruel days who had not courage for the fight— who sacrificed, and went their way. Not so these weak women.

"Once again they brought Perpetua her little child to try to shake her constancy. 'The prison was like a palace,' she said, while its little downy head lay on her breast. Her father wept, and even struck her in his grief and anger. 'I am a Christian,' she said, and gave him back the babe.

"They were thrown to the wild beasts. Felicitas and Perpetua, who had been tossed by a wild cow, though horribly gored, were still alive. Gladiators were summoned to behead them. Felicitas died at the first stroke, but the man's hand trembled, and he struck at Perpetua again and again, wounding her, but not mortally. 'You are more afraid than I,' she said gently and, taking the point of the sword, held it to her throat. 'Strike now,' she said, and so passed into the presence of her God."

Monica drew a long breath. "So weak and yet so strong," she said.

"So it is, my child," said the old woman. "It is those who are strong and true in the little things of life who are strong and true in the great trials."

"It is hard to be always strong and true," said the girl.

"Not if God's love comes always first," answered the old woman.

Monica was silent. She was thinking of her own young life, and how, with all the safeguards of a Christian home about her, she had narrowly escaped a great danger. From her babyhood she had been brought up by her father's old nurse— not over-tenderly, perhaps, but wisely, for the city of Tagaste was largely pagan in its habits, and the faithful old servant knew well what temptations would surround her nursling in later years. Monica, though full of life and spirit, had common sense and judgment beyond her years. She had also a great love of God and of all that belonged to His holy service, and would spend hours kneeling in the church in a quiet corner.

It was there she brought all her childish troubles and her childish hopes; it was to the invisible Friend in the sanctuary that she confided all the secrets of her young heart, and, above all, that desire to suffer for Him and for His Church with which the stories of the martyrs had inspired her. When the time slipped away too fast, and she returned home late, she accepted humbly the correction that awaited her, for she knew that she had disobeyed—although unintentionally—her nurse's orders.

Monica had been willfully disobedient once, and all her life long she would never forget the lesson her disobedience had taught her. It was a rule of her old nurse that she should take nothing to drink between meals, even in the hot days of summer in that sultry climate. If she had not courage to bear so slight a mortification as that, the old woman would argue, it would go ill with her in the greater trials of life. Monica had become used to the habit, but when she was old enough to begin to learn the duties of housekeeping her mother had desired that she should go every day to the cellar to draw the wine for the midday meal. A maid-servant went with her to carry the flagon, and the child, feeling delightfully important, filled and refilled the little cup which was used to draw the wine from the cask and emptied it carefully into the wine jar. When all was finished, a few drops remaining in the cup, a spirit of mischief took sudden possession of Monica and she drained it off, making a wry face as she did so at the strange taste. The maid-servant laughed, and continued to laugh when the performance was repeated the next day and the day after. The strange taste became gradually less strange and less unpleasant to the young girl; daily a few drops were added, until at last, scarcely thinking what she did, she would drink nearly the fill of the little cup, while the servant laughed as of old.

Monica was quick and intelligent and was learning her household duties well. Finding one day that a piece of work which fell to the lot of the maid who went with her to the wine cellar was very badly done, she reproved her severely. The woman turned on her young mistress angrily.

"It is not for a wine-bibber like you to find fault with me!" she retorted.

Monica stood horrified. The woman's insolent word had torn the veil from her eyes. Whither was she drifting? Into what depths might that one act of disobedience so lightly committed have led her had not God in His mercy intervened? She never touched wine for the rest of her life unless largely diluted with water. God had taught her that "he who despises small things shall fall by little and little," and Monica had learned the lesson. She had learned to distrust herself, and self-distrust makes one marvellously gentle with others; she had learned, too, to put her trust in God, and trust in God makes one marvellously strong. She had been taught to love the poor and the suffering, and to serve them at her own expense and inconvenience, and the service of others makes one unselfish. God had work for Monica to do in His world, as He has for us all if we will only do it, and He had given her what was needful for her task.

That night on the way to her chamber, as the young girl passed the place where she had sat with her grandmother earlier in the day, she paused a moment and looked out between the tall pillars into the starlit night, where the palm trees stood like dark shadows against the deep, deep blue of the sky. She clasped her hands, and her lips moved in prayer. "O God," she murmured, "to suffer for Thee and for Thy Faith!" God heard the whispered prayer, and He was to answer it later. There is a living martyrdom as painful and as bitter as death, and Monica was called to taste it.

Chapter 2

WIFE OF A PAGAN

ALTHOUGH there were many Christians in Roman Africa, pagan manners and customs still survived in many of her cities. The people clung to their games in the circus, the cruel and bloody combats of the arena, which, though forbidden by Constantine, were still winked at by provincial governors. They scarcely pretended to believe in their religion, but they held to the old pagan festivals, which enabled them to enjoy themselves without restraint under pretense of honoring the gods. The paganism of the fourth century, with its motto, "Let us eat, drink, and be merry," imposed no self-denial; it was therefore bound to be popular.

But unrestrained human nature is a dangerous thing. If men are content to live as the beasts that perish, they fall as far below their level as God meant them to rise above it—or rather, far further—and the Roman Empire was falling to pieces through its own corruption. In Africa the worship of the old Punic gods, to

9

whom living children used to be offered in sacrifice, still had its votaries, and priests of Sat-
urn and Astarte, with their long hair and painted
faces and scarlet robes, were still to be met danc-
ing madly in procession through the streets of
Carthage.

The various heretical sects had their preachers everywhere, proclaiming that there were much
easier ways of serving Christ than that taught
by the Catholic Church. It was hard for the
Christian bishops to keep their flocks untainted,
for there were enemies on every side.

When Monica was twenty-two years old her
parents gave her in marriage to a citizen of
Tagaste called Patricius. He held a good position in the town, for he belonged to a family
which, though poor, was noble. Monica knew
little of her future husband, save that he was
nearly twice her age and a pagan, but it was the
custom for parents to arrange all such matters,
and she had only to obey.

A little surprise was perhaps felt in Tagaste
that such good Christians should choose a pagan
husband for their beautiful daughter, but it was
found impossible to shake their hopeful views
for the future. When it was objected that Patricius was well known for his violent temper even
among his own associates, they answered that he
would learn gentleness when he became a Chris-

tian. That things might go hard with their daughter in the meantime they did not seem to foresee.

Monica took her new trouble where she had been used to take the old. Kneeling in her favorite corner in the church, she asked help and counsel of the Friend who never fails. She had had her girlish ideals of love and marriage. She had dreamed of a strong arm on which she could lean, of a heart and soul that would be at one with her in all that was most dear, of two lives spent together in God's love and service. And now it seemed that it was she who would have to be strong for both; to strive and to suffer to bring her husband's soul out of darkness into the light of truth. Would she succeed? And if not, what would be that married life which lay before her? She did not dare to think. She must not fail—and yet . . . "Thou in me, O Lord," she prayed again and again through her tears.

It was late when she made her way homeward, and that night, kneeling at her bedside, she laid the ideals of her girlhood at the feet of Him who lets no sacrifice, however small, go unrewarded. She would be true to this new trust, she resolved, cost what it might.

Things certainly did not promise well for the young bride's happiness. Patricius lived with his mother, a woman of strong passions like himself, and devoted to her son. She was bitterly jealous of the young girl who had stolen his affections and she made up her mind to dislike her. The slaves of the household followed, of course, their mistress's lead, and tried to please her by inventing stories against Monica.

Patricius, who loved his young wife with the only kind of love of which he was capable, had nothing in common with her, and had no clue to her thoughts or actions. He had neither reverence nor respect for women—indeed, most of the women of his acquaintance were deserving of neither—and he had chosen Monica for her beauty, much as he would have chosen a horse or a dog.

He thought her ways and ideas extraordinary. She took as kindly an interest in the slaves as if they had been of her own flesh and blood, and would even intercede to spare them a beating. She liked the poor, and would gather these dirty and unpleasant people about her, going even so far as to wash and dress their sores. Patricius did not share her attraction and objected strongly to such proceedings, but Monica pleaded so humbly and sweetly that he gave way and let her do what seemed to cause her so much pleasure.

There was "no accounting for tastes," he remarked. She would spend hours in the church praying, with her great eyes fixed on the altar. True, she was never there at any time when she was likely to be missed by her husband, and never was she so full of tender affection for him as when she came home; but still, it was a strange way of spending one's time.

There was something about Monica, it is true, that was altogether unlike any other inmate of the house, as she went about her daily duties, always watching for the chance of doing a kind action.

When Patricius was in one of his violent tempers, shouting, abusing and even striking everybody who came in his way, she would look at him with gentle eyes that showed neither fear nor anger. She never answered sharply, even though his rude words wounded her cruelly. He had once raised his hand to strike her, but he had not dared; something—he did not know what—withheld him.

Later, when his anger had subsided, and he was perhaps a little ashamed of his violence, she would meet him with an affectionate smile, forgiving and forgetting all. Only if he spoke himself, and, touched at her generous forbearance, tried shamefacedly to make amends for his treatment of her, would she gently explain her conduct. More often she said nothing, knowing that actions speak more loudly than words. As her greatest biographer says of her: "She spoke little, preached not at all, loved much and prayed unceasingly."

When the young wives of her acquaintance, married like herself to pagan husbands, complained of the insults and even blows which they had to bear, she would ask them laughingly, "Are you sure your own tongue is not to blame?" And then with ready sympathy she would do all she could to help and comfort and advise. They would ask her secret, for everyone knew that, in spite of the violence of Patricius' temper, he treated her with something that almost approached respect. Then she would bid them be patient, and love and pray, and meet harshness with gentleness, and abuse with silence. And when they sometimes answered that it would seem weak to knock under in such a fashion, Monica would ask them if they thought it needed more strength to speak or to be silent when provoked, and which was easier, to smile or to sulk when insulted? Many homes were happier in consequence, for Monica had a particular gift for making peace and even as a child had settled the quarrels of her young companions to everybody's satisfaction.

To the outside world Patricius' young wife seemed contented and happy. She managed her affairs well, people said, and no one but God

knew of the suffering that was her secret and
His. Brought up in the peace and piety of a
Christian family, she had had no idea of the
miseries of paganism. Now she had ample oppor-
tunity to study the effects of unchecked selfish-
ness and of uncontrolled passions; to see how
low human nature, unrestrained by faith and
love, could fall. Her mother-in-law treated her
with suspicion and dislike, for the slaves, never
weary of inventing fresh stories against her, mis-
represented all her actions to their mistress. Monica did not seem to notice unkindness, repaying
the many insults she received with little services
tactfully rendered, but she felt it deeply.

"They do not know," she would say to herself, and pray for them all the more earnestly,
offering her sufferings for these poor souls who
were so far from the peace of Christ. How was
the light to come to them if not through her?
How could they learn to love Christ unless they
learned to love His servants and to see Him in
them? The revelation must come through her, if
it was to come at all. "Thou in me, O Lord,"
she would pray, and draw strength and courage
at His feet for the daily suffering.

The heart of Patricius was like a neglected
garden. Germs of generosity, of nobility, lay hidden under a rank growth of weeds that no one
had ever taken any trouble to clear away. The

habits of a lifetime held him captive. With Monica he was always at his best, but he grew weary of being at his best. It was so much easier to be at his worst. He gradually began to seek distractions among his old pagan companions in the old ignoble pleasures.

The whole town began to talk of his neglect of his beautiful young wife. Monica suffered cruelly, but in silence. When he was at home, which was but seldom, she was serene and gentle as usual. She never reproached him, but treated him with the same tender deference as of old. Patricius felt the charm of her presence; all that was good in him responded; but evil habits had gone far to stifle the good, and his lower nature cried out for base enjoyments. He was not strong enough to break the chain which held him.

So Monica wept and prayed in secret, and God sent a ray of sunshine to brighten her sad life. Three children were born to her during the early years of her marriage. The name of Augustine, her eldest son, will be forever associated with that of his mother. Of the other two Navigius and Perpetua his sister, we know little. Navigius, delicate in health, was of a gentle and pious nature. Both he and Perpetua married, but the latter entered a monastery after her husband's death. With her younger children Monica had no trouble; it was the eldest, Augus tine, who, after having been for so long the son of her sorrow and of her prayers, was destined to be at last her glory and her joy.

Chapter 3

THE YOUNG AUGUSTINE

AS soon as the little Augustine was born, his mother had him taken to the Christian Church, that the Sign of the Cross might be made on his forehead and that he might be entered among the catechumens. It was a custom of the time—never approved of by the Church—to put off Baptism until the catechumen had shown himself able to withstand the temptations of the half-pagan society in the midst of which he had to live. Through this mistaken idea of reverence for the Sacrament, the young soldier of Christ, lest he should tarnish his weapons in the fight, was sent unarmed into a conflict in which he needed all the strength which the Sacraments alone can give.

The outlook for Monica, with her pagan husband and her pagan household, was darker than for most Christian mothers. Her heart grew heavy within her as she held her young son in her arms and thought of the future. For the present, indeed, he was hers; but later, when she could no longer keep him at her side and surround him with a mother's love and protection, what dangers would beset him? The influence of an unbelieving father during the years when his boyish ideas of life would be forming, a household that knew not Christ—how could he pass untouched through the dangers that would assail his young soul? With prayers and tears Monica bent over the unconscious little head that lay so peacefully upon her breast, commending her babe to the Heavenly Father, to whom all things are possible.

Augustine drank in the love of Christ with his mother's milk, he tells us. As soon as he could speak, she taught him to lisp a prayer. As soon as he could understand, she taught him, in language suited to his childish sense, the great truths of the Christian Faith. He would listen eagerly, and, standing at his mother's knee, or nestling in her arms, follow the sweet voice that could make the highest things so simple to his childish understanding.

It was the seed-time that was later to bear such glorious fruit, though the long days of winter lay between. The boy was thoughtful and intelligent; he loved all that was great and good and noble. The loathing of what was mean and base and unlovely, breathed into him by his mother in those days of early childhood, haunted

F. Ross Maguire

The little Augustine learns to know Jesus Christ.

him even during his worst moments in later life. The cry that burst from his soul in manhood when he had drunk deeply of the cup of earthly joys and found it bitter and unsatisfying had its origin in those early teachings. "Thou hast made us for Thyself, O Lord, and our hearts are restless until they rest in Thee."

One day, when the child was about seven years old, he was suddenly seized with sickness. He was in great pain and soon became so ill that his life was in danger. His parents were in anguish, but Augustine's one thought was for his soul; he begged and prayed that he might receive Baptism. Monica added her entreaties to his. Patricius yielded. All was prepared, when the child suddenly got better. Then someone intervened, probably his father, for Augustine tells us that the Baptism was put off again—indefinitely.

But it was time to think of the boy's education, and it was proposed to send him to school in Tagaste. It was a pagan school to which the child must go, pagan authors that he must study, and, worse than all, pagan conversation that he must hear and pagan playmates with whom he must associate.

Patricius was proud of the beauty and the intelligence of his little son and hoped great things for the future, but Augustine's early school days were far from brilliant. Eager as the boy was to learn what interested him, he had an insurmountable dislike to anything that caused him trouble. It bored him to learn to read and write, and the uninspiring truth that two and two make four was a weariness of the flesh to him. Though the stories of Virgil enchanted him, Homer he never thoroughly enjoyed nor quite forgave, for had he not for Homer's sake been forced to wade through the chilly waters of the Greek grammar?

Unfortunately for Augustine, such dismal truths as two and two make four have to be mastered before higher flights can be attempted. The Tagaste schoolmasters had but one way of sharpening their scholars' zeal for learning—the liberal use of the rod.

Now, Augustine disliked beatings as much as he disliked all other unpleasant things, but he also disliked work. The only way of evading both disagreeables was to follow the example of the greater number of his fellow scholars—to play when he should have been working, and to tell clever lies to his schoolmasters and his parents in order to escape punishment. Such tricks, however, are bound to be found out sooner or later, and Monica, realizing that much could be gotten out of her son by love, but little by fear, took him for a course of instruction to the Christian priests, that he might learn to overcome himself for the love of God.

As a result Augustine took more earnestly to his prayers, asking, above all, however, that he might not be beaten at school. His mother, finding him one day praying in a quiet corner to this intent, suggested that if he had learned his lessons for the day he need have no fear, but if he had not, punishment was to be expected. Patricius, who was passing and overheard the conversation, laughed at his son's fears and agreed with his wife. Augustine thought them both exceedingly heartless.

As the boy grew older, however, his wonderful gifts began to show themselves, and his masters, seeing of what he was really capable, punished him yet more severely when he was idle. Augustine, too, began to take pride in his own success and to wish to be first among his young companions. The latter cheated as a matter of course, both in work and at play. Bad habits are catching, and Augustine would sometimes cheat too. When found out he would fly into a passion, although no one was so severe on the dishonesty of others as he. And yet, though he would often yield to the temptations that were the hardest for his pleasure-loving nature to resist, there was much that was good in the boy. He had a faithful and loving heart, an attraction for all that was great and noble.

He was, in fact, his mother's son as well as his father's; the tares and the wheat were sprouting side by side.

But Augustine, at fourteen, was rapidly growing out of childhood. Patricius, prouder than ever of his clever son, resolved to spare no pains to give him the best education that his means could procure. The boy had a great gift of eloquence, said his masters, and much judgment; he would be certain to succeed brilliantly in the legal profession. It was decided to send him to Madaura, a town about twenty miles distant, a good deal larger than Tagaste and well known for its culture and its schools. It was one of the most pagan of the cities of Africa, but this was an objection that had no weight with Patricius, although it meant much to Monica. The only comfort for her in this first separation was the thought that there at least her son would not be far from home. In truth, not far away as distance goes, but how far away in spirit!

Madaura was a large and handsome city with a circus and theatre and a fine forum, or marketplace, set round with statues of the gods. It was proud of its reputation for learning, but had little else to be proud of. Its professors were men who were more ashamed of being detected in a fault of style than in the grossest crimes—who were ashamed, indeed, of nothing else. The pagan gods were held up to their scholars as models for admiration and imitation.

It was a poor ideal at the best. The gods were represented by the great pagan poets and authors as no better, if more powerful, than ordinary mortals. They were described as subject to all the meannesses and all the baseness of the least noble of their worshippers. That their supposed adventures, neither moral nor elevating, were told in the most exquisite language by the greatest authors of antiquity rather added to the danger than decreased it. True, the noblest of the classical writers broke away continually from the bondage which held them, to stretch out groping hands towards the eternal truth and beauty into which real genius must always have some insight, but not all were noble.

The students of Madaura were worthy of their masters. Nothing was too shameful to be talked about, if only it were talked about in well-turned phrases. The plays acted in the theatre were what might be expected in Roman society of the fourth century—that society from which St. Antony and St. Jerome had been forced to flee to the desert in order to save their souls.

Augustine won golden opinions from his masters for his quickness and intelligence. They thought of nothing else but of cultivating the minds of their scholars. Heart and soul were left untouched, or touched in such a way that evil sprang to life and good was stifled. Augustine was a genius, they cried, a budding rhetorician, a poet!

Although masters and scholars alike applauded him, Augustine, while he drank their praises greedily, was restless and unhappy. He had gone down before the subtle temptations of Madaura like corn before the scythe. First evil thoughts, but carelessly resisted; then evil deeds. He had lost his childish innocence, and with it his childish happiness. For he knew too much, and was too noble of nature, to be easily content with what was ignoble. The seeds of his mother's teaching were yet alive within him.

And Monica? Only twenty miles away at Tagaste she was praying for her son, beseeching the Heavenly Father to keep him from evil, to watch over him now that she was no longer at his side, hoping and trusting that all was well with her boy.

Chapter 4

NEW JOYS, NEW SORROW

MONICA, it is true, was a Saint, but a Saint in the making. Saints are not born ready-made; holiness is a beautiful thing that is built up stone by stone, not brought into being by the touch of the enchanter's wand.

During the years that had passed since Patricius had brought his young wife home to his mother's house, Monica would have been the first to confess how far she had fallen short of the ideal she had set herself to attain. Yet there had been ceaseless effort, ceaseless prayer, unwearying love and patience. And God was sending many actual graces to the souls in this pagan household.

The mother of Patricius was growing old; she was neither so active nor so strong as she had been. What had used to be easy to her was becoming difficult. It galled her independent spirit to be obliged to ask help of others. Monica, reading her heart as only the unselfish can, saw this and understood. At every moment the older woman would find that some little service had been done by unseen hands, some little thoughtful act that made things easier for the tired old limbs. There was someone who seemed to know and understand what she wanted almost before she did herself.

Who could it be? Not the slaves, certainly. They did their duty for fear of being beaten, but that was all. It was all, indeed, that was expected of them. Not Patricius, either; it was not his way, he never thought of such things. It could therefore be no one but Monica.

The old woman mused deeply. She had treated her daughter-in-law harshly and unkindly during all these years. She had looked upon her as an intruder. But then, the slaves had told her unpleasant stories of their young mistress; it was only what Monica deserved. And yet . . . It was hard to think of those ugly tales in connection with Monica as she herself knew her—as she had seen her day by day since she first came, a young bride, to her husband's home.

Again, how had Monica repaid her for her unkindness? With never-failing charity and sweetness, with gentle respect and deference to her wishes, never trying to assert herself, never appealing to her husband to give her the place which of right belonged to her. She had been content to be treated as the last in the house.

The old woman sat lost in thought. What would the house be like, she suddenly asked herself, without that gentle presence? What would she do, what would they all do, without Monica? With a sudden pang of sorrow she realized how much she leaned upon her daughter-in-law and what her life would be without her. She considered the matter in this new light. She was a woman of strong passions but also of sound common sense; reason was beginning to triumph over prejudice.

Sending for the slaves, she questioned them sharply as to the tales they had told her about their young mistress. They faltered, contradicted each other and themselves and in the end confessed that they had lied.

The old lady went straight to her son and told him the whole story. Patricius was not one to take half measures in such a matter. Not even the petitions of Monica, all unconscious of the particular offense they had committed, availed to save the culprits. They were as soundly beaten as they had ever been in their lives, after which they were told that they knew what to expect if they ever breathed another word against their young mistress again. As it happened, they had no desire to do so. The hidden forces of grace had been working there too. Monica's kindness, her sympathy with their joys and sorrows—to them something strange and new—had already touched their hearts. More than once they had been sorry for ever having spoken against her; they had felt ashamed in her presence.

Justice having been done regarding the slaves, the mother of Patricius sought out her daughter-in-law, told her frankly that she had been in the wrong and asked her forgiveness. Monica clasped the old woman in her arms and refused to listen. From that moment they were the truest of friends.

There were many things to be spoken of, but first, religion. Monica had revealed her Faith by her life, her daily actions, and to the other it was a beautiful and alluring revelation. She wanted to know, to understand; she listened eagerly to Monica's explanations.

It was a message of new life, of hope beyond the grave, of joy, of peace; she begged to be received as a catechumen. It was not long before she knelt at Monica's side before the altar to be signed on the brow with the Cross of Christ— the joyous first fruits of the seed that had been sown in tears.

One by one the slaves followed their mistress' example, hungering in their turn for the message that brought such peace and light to suffering and weary souls. Was it for such as they? they asked. And Monica answered that it was for all, that the Master Himself had chosen to be as one who served.

The whole household was Christian now, with the exception of Patricius, and even he was growing daily more gentle, more thoughtful. The mysterious forces of grace were working on him too. His love for Monica was more reverent; his eyes were opening slowly to the beauty of spiritual things. The old life, with its old pleasures, was growing distasteful to him; he saw its baseness while as yet he could scarcely tear himself free from its fetters—the fetters of old habit so hard to break. He noticed the change in his mother and half envied her her courage. He even envied the slaves their happy faces, the new light that shone in their eyes and that gave them a strange new dignity.

Monica, watching the struggle, redoubled her prayers; her unselfish love surrounded her husband like an atmosphere of light and sweetness. She would speak to him of their children—above all, of Augustine, their eldest-born, the admiration of his masters at Madaura. He was astonishing everybody, they wrote, by his brilliant gifts. He had the soul of a poet and the eloquence of an orator; he would do great things.

Madaura had been all very well up till now, his father decided, but everything must be done to give their boy a good start in life; they must go further. Rome was impossible; the distance was too great and the expense too heavy. Patricius' means were limited, but he resolved to do his utmost for his eldest son.

Carthage had a reputation for culture and for learning that was second only to that of Rome. If strict economy were practiced at home, Carthage might be possible. In the meantime, it was not much use leaving the boy at Madaura. Let him come home and remain there a year, during which he could study privately while they saved the money to pay his expenses at Carthage.

The suggestion delighted Monica. She would have her son with her for a whole year. She would be able to watch over him just when he needed her motherly care; she looked forward eagerly to Augustine's return. The old, intimate life they had led together before he went to Madaura would begin again. Again her son would tell her all his hopes and dreams for the future. She would look once more into the boy's clear eyes while he confessed to her his faults and failings, and see the light flame up in them as she told him of noble and heroic deeds and urged him to be true to high ideals. And so in happy dreams the days went past until Augustine's return.

But there was bitter grief in store for Monica. This was not the same Augustine that they had left at Madaura two years ago. The days of the old familiar friendship seemed to have gone past recall. His eyes no longer turned to her with the old candor; he shunned her questioning look. He even shunned her company and seemed more at ease with his father, who was proud beyond words of his tall, handsome son.

He was all right, said Patricius; he was growing up, that was all. Boys could not always be tied to their mother's apron-strings. The moment that Monica had so dreaded for Augustine had come, then; the pagan influences had been at work. Oh, why had she let him go to Madaura? And yet it had to be so; his father had insisted.

She made several efforts to break through the wall of reserve that Augustine had built up between himself and her, but it was of no use. He had other plans now, into which she did not enter, other thoughts far away—how far away!—from hers. A dark cloud was between them.

One day she persuaded her son to go out walking with her. The spring had just come—that wonderful African spring when the whole world seems suddenly to burst into flower. Asphodels stood knee-deep on either side of the path in which they walked, the fragrance of the springtime was in their nostrils, the golden sunlight bathed the rainbow earth. It was a walk that they had loved to take of old, to delight together in all the beauty of that world which God had made.

Monica spoke gently to her son of the new life that lay before him, of the dangers that beset his path. He must hold fast to the Law of Christ, she told him; he must be pure and strong and true.

There was no answering gleam as of old. The boy listened with a bad grace; shame and honor were tugging at his heart-strings, but in vain. The better self was defeated, for the lower self was growing stronger every day.

"Woman's talk," he said to himself. "I am no longer a child."

They turned back through the glorious sights and sounds of the springtime; there was a dagger in Monica's heart. On the threshold she met Patricius. He wanted to speak to her, he said. She slipped her arm into his, smiling through her pain, and they went back again, between the nodding asphodels and the hedges of wisteria, along the path she had just trodden with her son.

There was an unwonted seriousness about Patricius. He had been thinking deeply of late, he told her. He had begun to see things in a new light. It was dim as yet, and he was still weak; but the old life and the pagan religion had grown hateful to him. Her God was the true God; he

F. Ross Maguire

Patricius tells his wife of his desire to be a Christian.

wanted to know how to love and serve that God of hers. Was he fit, did she think, to learn? Could he be received as a catechumen?

The new joy fell like balm on the new sorrow. Monica had lost her son, but gained her husband. God was good. He had heard her prayers, He had accepted her sacrifice. Surely He would also give her back her son. She would trust on and hope. "He will withhold no good thing from them that ask Him."

A few days later Patricius knelt beside Monica at the altar. Her heart overflowed with joy and thankfulness. They were one at last—one in soul, in faith.

A few steps distant knelt Augustine. What thoughts were in his heart? Was it the struggle between good and evil? Was the influence of his mother, the love of Christ she had instilled into him in his childhood, making one last stand against the influences that had swayed him in Madaura—that still swayed him—the influences of the corrupt world in which he lived? We do not know. If it was so, the evil triumphed.

Chapter 5

SON TO CARTHAGE, HUSBAND TO ETERNITY

AUGUSTINE'S year at home did not do for him what Monica had hoped. His old pagan schoolfellows gathered round him; he was always with them; the happy home life seemed to have lost its charm. The want of principle and of honor in most of Augustine's friends disgusted him in his better moments; nevertheless, he was content to enjoy himself in their company. He was even ashamed, when they boasted of their misdoings, to seem more innocent than they, and would pretend to be worse than he really was, lest his prestige should suffer in their eyes. There were moments when he loathed it all and longed for the old life with its innocent pleasures, but it is hard to turn back on the downhill road.

Augustine tells in his *Confessions* how he went one night with a band of these wild companions to rob the fruit tree of a poor neighbor. It was laden with pears, but they were not very good. The youths did not care to eat them, so they threw them to the pigs. It was not school-boy greed that prompted the theft, but the pure delight of doing evil, of tricking the owner of the garden. There was the wild excitement, too, of the daring, the fear that they might be caught in the act. Augustine was careful to keep such escapades a secret from his mother, but Monica was uneasy, knowing what might be expected from the companions her son had chosen.

Patricius was altogether unable to give Augustine the help that he needed. The Christian ideals of life and conduct were new to him as yet, the old pagan ways seemed only natural. He was scarcely likely to be astonished at the fact that his son's boyhood was rather like what his own had been. He was standing, it is true, on the threshold of the Church, but her teaching was not yet clear to him. His own feet were not firm enough in the ways of Christ to enable him to stretch a steadying hand to another.

Patricius' mother was failing fast; the end could not be far off. Monica was devoting herself heart and soul to the old woman, who clung to her with tender affection and was never happy in her absence.

Patricius watched them together and marvelled at the effects of the grace of Baptism. Was that indeed his mother, he asked himself, that gentle, patient old woman, so thoughtful for others, so ready to give up her own will? She had used to be violent and headstrong like himself, resentful and implacable in her dislikes, but now she was more like Monica than like him. That was Monica's way, though; her sweetness and patience seemed to be catching. She was like the sunshine, penetrating everywhere with its light and warmth. He, alas! was far behind his mother. Catechumen though he was, the old temper would often flash out still. Self-conquest was the hardest task that he had ever undertaken, and sometimes he almost lost heart and was inclined to give it up altogether. Then Monica would gently remind him that with God's help the hardest things were possible, and they would kneel and pray together, and Patricius would take heart again for the fight.

Monica had a wonderful gift for giving people courage; Patricius had noticed that before. He supposed it was because she was so full of sympathy and always made allowances. And then she seemed to think—to be sure, even—that if one went on trying, failures did not matter, God did not mind them; and that was a very comforting reflection for poor, weak people like himself. To go on trying was possible even for him, although he knew he could not always promise himself success.

Patricius was anxious about Augustine's future. All his efforts had not succeeded in saving the sum required for his first year at Carthage. He had discovered that it would cost a good deal more than he had at first supposed, and it was difficult to see where the money was to come from.

It was at this moment that Romanianus, a wealthy and honorable citizen of Tagaste, who knew the poverty of his friend, came forward generously and put his purse at Patricius' disposal. The sum required was offered with such delicacy that it could not be declined. Augustine was sure to bring glory on his native town, said Romanianus; it was an honor to be allowed to help in his education.

Monica was almost glad to see her son depart. He was now seventeen. The old boyish laziness had given way to a real zeal for learning and thirst after knowledge. The idle life at home was certainly the worst thing for him. Hard work and the pursuit of wisdom might steady his wild nature and bring him back to God. This was her hope now, as with prayers and tears she besought Him to watch over her son.

But Monica did not know Carthage. If it was second only to Rome for its culture and its schools, it almost rivaled Rome in its corruption. There all that was worst in the civilization of the East and of the West met and mingled. The bloody combats between men and beasts, the gladiatorial shows that delighted the Romans, were free to all who chose to frequent the amphitheatre of Carthage. Such plays as the Romans delighted in, impossible to describe, were acted in the theatre. The horrible rites of the Eastern religions were practiced openly.

There was neither discipline nor order in the schools. The wealthier students gloried in their bad reputation. They were young men of fashion who were capable of anything, and who were careful to let others know it. They went by the name of "smashers" or "upsetters," from their habit of raiding the schools of professors whose teaching they did not approve and breaking everything on which they could lay hands. They treated newcomers with coarse brutality, though Augustine seems in some manner to have escaped their enmity. Perhaps a certain dignity in the young man's bearing, or perhaps his brilliant gifts, won their respect, for he surpassed them all in intelligence and speedily outstripped them in class.

Augustine was eager for knowledge and eager for enjoyment. He frequented the theatre; his pleasure-loving nature snatched at everything that life could give, yet he was not happy. "My God," he cried in later years, "with what bitter gall didst Thou in Thy great mercy sprinkle those pleasures of mine!" He could not forget; and at Tagaste his mother was weeping and praying for her son.

Patricius prayed with her; he understood at last. Every day the germs of a noble nature that had lain so long dormant within him were gaining strength and life. Every day, with grace, his soul was opening more and more to the understanding of spiritual things, while Monica watched the transformation with a heart that overflowed with gratitude and love. The sorrows of the past were all forgotten in the joy of the present, that happy union at the feet of Christ.

There was but one cause for sadness—Patricius' health was failing. His mother had already shown him the joys of a Christian deathbed. She had passed away smiling, with their hands in hers, and the name of Jesus on her lips. The beautiful prayers of the Church had gone down with the departing soul to the threshold of the new life and had followed it into eternity. She seemed close to them still in the light of that wonderful new Faith, and to be waiting for them in their everlasting home.

But Monica's happiness was to be short-lived, for it seemed that Patricius would soon rejoin his mother. He did not deceive himself. He spoke of his approaching death to Monica and asked her to help him to make a worthy preparation for Baptism, which he desired to receive as soon as possible. With the simplicity and trustfulness of a child, he looked to her for guidance and did all that she desired.

The day of Baptism came. The ceremony over, Patricius turned to his wife and smiled. A wonderful peace possessed him. The old life, with all its stains, had passed from him in those cleansing waters; the new life was at hand. Once more he asked her to forgive him all the pain he had caused her, all that he had made her suffer. She must not grieve, he told her; the parting would be but for a little while, the meeting for all eternity. She had been his angel, he said; he owed all his joy to her. It was her love, her patience, that had done it all. She had shown him the beauty of goodness and made him love it. He thanked her for all that she had been to him, all that she had shown him, all that she had done for him. Monica's tears fell on Patricius' face, her loving arms supported him; her sweet voice, broken with weeping, spoke words of hope and comfort.

On the threshold of that other world Monica bade farewell to her husband, and one more soul that she had won for Christ went out to a glorious eternity.

Chapter 6

AUGUSTINE AT CARTHAGE

PATRICIUS had not much in the way of worldly goods to leave to his wife. She needed little, it is true, for herself, but there was Augustine. Would it be possible for her, even if she practiced the strictest economy, to keep him at Carthage, where he was doing so well?

Romanianus divined her anxiety and hastened to set it at rest. He had a house in Carthage, he said; it should be Augustine's as long as he required it. This would settle the question of lodging. For the rest, continued Romanianus, as an old friend of Patricius he had the right to befriend his son, and Monica must grant him the privilege of acting a father's part to Augustine until he was fairly launched in life. He had a child of his own, a young son called Licentius. If Monica would befriend his boy, they would be even. The gratitude of both mother and son toward this generous friend and benefactor lasted throughout their lives. Licentius was to feel its effects more than once.

"You it was, Romanianus," wrote Augustine in his *Confessions*, "who, when I was a poor young student in Carthage, opened to me your house, your purse, and still more your heart. You it was who, when I had the sorrow to lose my father, comforted me by your friendship, helped me with your advice and assisted me with your fortune."

Monica mourned her husband's death with true devotion, but hers was not a selfish sorrow. She had love and sympathy for all who needed them, and she forgot her own grief in solacing that of others. There were certain good works which the Church gave to Christian widows to perform. The hospitals, for instance, were entirely in their hands. These institutions were small as yet, built according to the needs of the moment from the funds of the faithful, and they held but few patients. These devoted women succeeded each other at intervals in their task of washing and attending to the sick, watching by their beds and cleaning their rooms. Their ministrations did not even cease there. With reverent care they prepared the dead for burial, thinking the while of the preparation of Christ's body for the tomb and of Him who said: "As long as you did it to one of these My least brethren, you did it to Me."

It was a happy moment for Monica when her

turn came to serve the sick. She would kiss their sores for very pity as she washed and dressed them, and their faces grew bright at her coming. They called her "Mother." It seemed such a natural name to give her, for she was a mother to them all and gave them a mother's love. To some of the poor creatures, friendless slaves as they often were, who had known little sympathy or tenderness in their hard lives, it was a revelation of Christianity which taught them more than hours of preaching could have done.

But there was other work besides that at the hospital. There were the poor to be helped, the hungry to be fed, the naked to be clothed. She would gather the orphan children at her knee to teach them the truths of their Faith. When they were very poor, she would keep them in her own house, feed them at her own table and clothe them with her own hands. "If I am a mother to these motherless ones," she would say to herself, "He will have mercy and give me back my boy; if I teach them to know and love Him as a Father, He will watch over my son."

It was a custom of the time on the feasts of Saints and Martyrs to make a pilgrimage to their tombs with a little basket of food and wine. This was laid on the grave, after which the faithful would partake of what they had brought, while they thought and spoke of the noble lives of God's servants who had gone before. The custom was abolished not long after, on account of the abuses which had arisen, but Monica observed it to the end. She scarcely tasted of her offering herself, but gave it all away to the poor. Often, indeed, she went cold and hungry that they might be clothed and fed.

Her love of prayer, too, could now find full scope. Every morning found her in her place in church for the Holy Sacrifice; every evening she was there again, silent, absorbed in God. The place where she knelt was often wet with her tears; the time passed by unheeded. Patricius, her husband, was safe in God's hands; but Augustine, her eldest-born, her darling, in what dark paths was he wandering? And yet in her heart there was a deep conviction that no sad news of his life at Carthage could shake. His was not the nature to find contentment in the things of earth. He was born to something higher. His noble heart, his strong intelligence, would bring him back to God.

And yet, and yet . . . her heart sank as she thought of graces wasted, of conscience trampled underfoot, of light rejected. No, there was no hope anywhere but with God. In Him she would trust, and in Him alone. He was infinite in mercy and strong to save. He had promised that He would never fail those who put their trust in Him.

At His feet, and at His feet alone, Monica poured out her tears and her sorrow. With others she was serene and hopeful as of old, even joyous, always ready to help and comfort. It was said of her after her death that no one had such a gift of helping others as she. She never preached at people—most people have an insurmountable dislike of being preached at—but every word she said had a strange power of drawing souls to God, of making them wish to be better.

Augustine, meanwhile, at Carthage, was justifying all the hopes that had been formed of him. He had even greater gifts, it seemed, than eloquence, feeling and wit. He was at the head of his class in rhetoric. His master had spoken to him of a certain treatise of Aristotle which he would soon be called upon to study. It was so profound, he said, that few could understand it, even with the help of the most learned professors. Augustine, eager to make acquaintance with this wonderful work, procured it at once and read it. It seemed to him perfectly simple; it was unnecessary, he found, to ask a single explanation.

It was the same with geometry, music, every science he took up. This young genius of nineteen only discovered there were difficulties in the way when he had to teach others and realized how hard it was to make them understand what was so exceedingly simple to himself.

There was something strangely sympathetic and attractive about Augustine. He seemed modest and reserved about his own gifts, although he himself tells us in his *Confessions* that he was full of pride and ambition. He had a gift of making true and faithful friends, a charm in conversation that drew his young companions, and even older men, to his side.

A more worldly mother than Monica would have been thoroughly proud of her son. Faith and virtue were alone weak and faint in that soul that could so ill do without them, but to her they were the one essential thing; the rest did not matter. Yet Monica, with true insight, believed that with noble minds knowledge must point men to God; she hoped much, therefore, that God would use Augustine's brilliance of intellect to save him in the end.

Already the noble philosophy of Cicero—pagan though he was—had awakened a thirst for wisdom in the young student's soul; already he felt the emptiness of earthly joys. "I longed, my God," he writes, "to fly from the things of earth to Thee, and I knew not that it was Thou that wast working in me . . ."

"One thing cooled my ardor," he goes on to say; "it was that the Name of Christ was not there; and this Name, by Thy mercy, Lord, of Thy Son, my Saviour, my heart had drawn in with my mother's milk and kept in its depths; and every doctrine where this Name did not appear—fluent, elegant and truth-like though it might be—could not master me altogether."

Augustine then turned to the Holy Scriptures, but they appeared to him inferior in style to Cicero. "My pride," he writes, "despised the manner in which the things are said, and my intelligence could not discover the hidden sense. They become great only for the humble, and I disdained to humble myself, and, inflated with vainglory, I believed myself great."

It was at this moment that Augustine came into contact with the Manichaeans, whose errors attracted him at once. This extraordinary heresy had begun in the East and had spread all over the civilized world. Its followers formed a secret society with signs and passwords, grades and initiations. To impose on Christians, they used Christian words for doctrines that were thoroughly unchristian. Perhaps the most remarkable thing about them was their hatred of the Church. Augustine, who remained among them for nine years, described them thus when writing to a friend:

"Thou knowest, Honoratus, that for this reason alone did we fall into the hands of these men—namely, that they professed to free us from all errors and bring us to God by pure reason alone, without that terrible principle of authority. For what else induced me to abandon the faith of my childhood and follow these men for almost nine years but their assertion that we were terrified by superstition into a faith blindly imposed upon our reason, while they urged no one to believe until the truth was fully discussed and proved? Who would not be seduced by such promises, especially if he were a proud, contentious young man, thirsting for truth, such as they then found me?"

That was what the Manichaeans promised. What Augustine actually found among them he also tells us:

"They incessantly repeated to me, 'Truth, truth,' but there was no truth in them. They taught what was false, not only about Thee, my God, Who art the very Truth, but even about the elements of this world, Thy creatures."

So much for their doctrines; as for the teachers themselves, Augustine found them "carnal and loquacious, full of insane pride."

The great charm of Manichaeism to Augustine was that it taught that a man was not responsible for his sins. This doctrine was convenient to one who could not find the strength to break with his bad habits.

"Such was my mind," he sums up later, looking back on this period of his life, "so weighed down, so blinded by the flesh, that I was myself unknown to myself."

Chapter 7

MONICA'S SON STRUGGLES IN DARKNESS

ILL news travels fast. Augustine had scarcely joined the Manichaeans before the tidings reached Monica. At first she could hardly believe it. This was a blow for which she had not been prepared; it crushed her to the earth. She would have grieved less over the news of her son's death.

And yet she bent her broken heart to God's will and hoped on in Him "whose mercy cannot fail." Augustine had renounced the Christian Faith publicly, she heard later; he had been entered by the Manichaeans as an "auditor," the first degree of initiation in their sect. And with all the zeal and ardor that he carried into everything he did, he was advocating this abominable heresy and persuading his companions to follow his example.

Monica's eyes grew dim with weeping for her son. He was dead indeed to God—that God who was her All in All.

The vacation was near, and Augustine would

then return to Tagaste. Perhaps she would find that it was not so bad as she had thought. It might be only the whim of a moment; she would wait and see.

Alas! the hope was vain. Augustine had scarcely been a day at home before he began obstinately to air his new opinions, determined that she should listen. Then the Christian in Monica rose above the mother; her horror of heresy showed itself stronger than her love for her son. Standing before him, outraged and indignant, Monica told Augustine plainly that if he spoke in such a way she could no longer receive him at her table or in her house.

Augustine was amazed; he had at last found out the limits of his mother's endurance. With bent head he left the house and sought the hospitality of Romanianus.

No sooner had he gone than Monica's heart melted, the mother-love surged up again. With bitter tears she cried out to God to help her; her grief seemed greater than she could bear. At last the night came, and with it peace. As Monica slept, exhausted with weeping, she had a dream which brought her a strange sense of hope and comfort.

It seemed to her that she was standing on a narrow rule or plank of wood, her heart weighed down with sorrow, as it had been all through the day. Suddenly there came toward her a young man radiant and fair of face. Smiling at her, he asked the cause of her tears. "I am weeping," she answered "for the loss of my son."

"Grieve no more, then," he replied, "for, look, your son is standing there beside you." Monica turned her head. It was true; Augustine stood at her side on the plank of wood. "Be of good cheer," continued the stranger, "for where you are, there shall he be also." Then Monica awoke; the words were ringing in her ears; it seemed to her that God had spoken.

In the morning she went straight to Augustine and told him of her dream. "Perhaps," suggested her son, anxious to turn it to his own advantage, "it means that you will come to see things as I do."

"No," said Monica firmly, "for he did not say, 'Where *he* is, *you* shall be,' but 'Where *you* are, there *he* shall be.'" Augustine was even more struck by the earnestness of his mother's answer than by the dream itself, though he pretended to make light of both.

Not long after, Monica went to see a certain holy bishop, that she might beg him to use his influence with Augustine to bring him back to the truth. The wise old man listened attentively to her story. "Let him alone for the present, but pray much," was his advice, "for as yet he is obstinate and puffed up with these new ideas. If what you tell me of your son is true, he will read for himself and will find out his error." Then, seeing the anguish of the poor mother, he told her that he himself in his youth had been led away by the Manichaeans and had even been employed in transcribing their works. It was that which had awakened him; for, as he wrote, the truth became clear to him; he had seen how much their doctrines were to be avoided. Then, as Monica wept for disappointment—for she had counted greatly on the Bishop's help— a sudden pity seized him. "Go thy way, and God bless thee!" he cried. "It is not possible that the son of so many tears should perish!"

Monica's dream and the words of the Bishop were like rays of light in the darkness. She drew fresh hope from them and redoubled her prayers.

The vacation drew to an end, and Augustine returned to Carthage, but not for long. He was now twenty years old. His friend and patron, Romanianus, was very anxious that Augustine should open a school in Tagaste while waiting for something better, and this he resolved to do. A little circle of pupils soon gathered round him, who were later to follow their young master in all his wanderings. Among these was Alypius, an old school-fellow and a devoted friend, the sons of Romanianus, and another friend of Augustine's childhood whose name we do not know but who was dearer to him than all the rest. They were of the same age, had studied together, had the same tastes and the same ambitions. Influenced by Augustine, still warm in the praise of the Manichaeans, he, as well as the rest, had abjured the Catholic Faith to join their heresy.

Augustine had been about a year at Tagaste when this friend was taken suddenly ill. He lay unconscious in a burning fever; there seemed to be no hope of recovery. He had been a catechumen before he had joined the Manichaeans. His Christian parents having begged that he might be baptized before he died, the life-giving waters were poured on him as he lay between life and death. Augustine made no protest, so sure was he that what he himself had taught this friend before he was taken ill would have more influence than a rite administered without his knowledge or consent. To everybody's surprise, the young man recovered his senses and began to mend.

Augustine then laughingly told him what had been done and went on to make fun of the whole proceeding, never doubting but that the sick man would enjoy the joke as much as he did. To his great surprise, his friend turned from him in horror.

"Never speak to me in such a way again if

you wish to keep my affection," he said.

"We will talk this matter out when you are stronger," thought Augustine. But a few days later, the invalid had a relapse and died with the white robe of his Baptism still unstained.

Augustine was inconsolable. Everything in Tagaste reminded him of the dear companion of his boyhood. "My own country became a punishment to me," he writes, "and my father's house a misery, and all places or things in which I had communicated with him were turned into a bitter torment to me, being now without him. My eyes sought him everywhere, and I hated all things because they had him not." The thought of death was full of horror to him, and he gave way to a deep depression. His health, never very robust, began to suffer.

Romanianus, much as he wished to keep Augustine at Tagaste, realized that a change of scene would be the best thing for him and agreed to his proposal to return to Carthage and open a school of rhetoric. Alypius and his other disciples followed him, and in the rush of the great city Augustine regained, to some extent, his peace of mind. While teaching, he continued his own studies and competed for the public prizes. Many men of note joined his school, and his name began to be famous.

He greatly desired honor, he tells us, but only

if honorably won. One day a certain magician paid him a visit. He had heard, he said, that Augustine was about to compete for one of the State prizes in rhetoric. What would he be ready to give if the magician could insure him the victory? It would only be necessary to offer some living creatures in sacrifice to the demons whom he worshipped, and success would be certain. Augustine turned from the magician in horror and disgust. He had not yet fallen so low as this.

"I would not sacrifice a fly," he retorted hotly, "to win a crown of gold!"

The magician retired in haste, and Augustine, who succeeded in carrying off the prize without the help of the demons, was publicly crowned by the Pro-Consul Vindicius, who from thenceforth joined the circle of Augustine's friends.

The news of his success reached Monica. Her mother's heart rejoiced in his triumph, but her joy was tempered with sorrow. Carthage had taken more from her son than it could ever give him, and her thoughts were of other victories and other crowns. During his stay in Tagaste, although Augustine had not lived under the same roof with his mother, he had been continually with her. Her tender affection had been his greatest comfort in the deep sorrow after his friend's death. He spoke no more to her of religion, and she, mindful of the old Bishop's words, was also silent.

"While I was struggling in the mire and in the darkness of error," writes Augustine, "that holy, chaste, devout and sober widow (such as Thou lovest) ceased not in all the hours of her prayers to bewail me in Thy sight. And her prayers were admitted into Thy presence, and yet Thou sufferedst me to go on still and to be involved in that darkness."

The darkness was indeed great, but the fires were still smoldering beneath the ashes. Honor, success and friendship were all his, and yet he was not content. There was something in his soul that none of these things could satisfy. "After Thee, O Truth," he cried, "I hungered and thirsted!"

Augustine's heart still ached for the loss of his friend. He turned everywhere for comfort, but found none. He sought forgetfulness in study. He wrote two books on the "Beautiful" and the "Apt," and dedicated them to Hierus, a famous Roman orator. "It seemed to me a great thing," he tells us, "that my style and my studies should be known to such a man."

Monica drew fresh hope from her son's writings. They were full of noble thoughts and high aspirations. Could such a mind remain in error? Some day, surely, by God's grace, in God's good time, Augustine would come to know the truth.

Chapter 8

MONICA'S HEARTBREAK

IT was about this time that Augustine's enthusiasm for the Manichaeans began to cool. He had been studying their doctrines and had found that they were not quite what he thought. He was disappointed with their professors too.

The first unpleasant truth that dawned upon him was that the Manichaeans were much better at denying the doctrines of the Catholic Church than at explaining their own. It was almost impossible to find out what they believed, so vague did they become when closely questioned. And Augustine questioned very closely indeed. He was on the track of truth, and it was not easy to put him off with hazy general statements. He was still only an "auditor," and before he took any further step he wanted to be certain of his ground. The men whom he consulted did not seem very certain of their own, he remarked, but they bade him have patience. One of their bishops, Faustus by name, was soon coming to Carthage. He was one of their most brilliant preachers and would be able to answer all Augustine's questions.

This sounded promising, and Augustine awaited the coming of Faustus impatiently. He certainly was an eloquent speaker; his sermons were charming. But when Augustine went to him privately and explained his doubts to him, the result was not what he had hoped for. Faustus gave the same vague answers that Augustine had so often heard already. Pressed closer, he frankly replied that he was not learned enough to be able to satisfy Augustine. Augustine was pleased with Faustus' honesty, and the two became good friends. But the seeker was no nearer the truth than before.

Yet if Faustus could not answer him, which of the Manichaeans could? Augustine began to lose faith in them.

What did the Catholic Church teach on these points? he asked. This was a question which they could all answer, and did—with great eagerness and little truth.

It might have occurred to a less intelligent man than Augustine that the enemies of the Church were not the people to answer such a question fairly or truthfully; but he accepted their rendition of the facts, and decided that truth was not to be found in the Catholic Church either. Was there such a thing as truth at all?

was the final question he asked himself. The old philosophers, heathens as they were, seemed to get nearer to the heart of things than this.

Yet now and again, out of the very sickness of his soul, a prayer would break out to that Christ whom he had known and loved in his boyhood but who had grown so dim to him since the Manichaeans had taught him that His Sacred Humanity was nothing but a shadow. Augustine was weary of life, weary even of pleasure, weary of everything, weary most of all of Carthage.

Owing to the wild ways of the students it was impossible to keep anything like order in the schools. Classes were constantly interrupted by gangs of "smashers" who might break in at any moment, setting the whole place in an uproar.

Augustine's friends pressed him to go to Rome. There, they urged, he would meet with the honor that he deserved. There the students were quieter and better-mannered; no rioting was allowed; scholars might enter no school but that of their own master. This sounded hopeful; Augustine was rather pleased with the idea. He wrote to Monica and to his patron Romanianus to tell them of the step he proposed to take.

Monica's heart sank when she read the letter. To the Christians of the fourth century, Rome was another Babylon. She had poured out the blood of the saints like water; she was the home of every abomination. What would become of Augustine in Rome? Without faith, without ideals, he was a disabled ship, drifting with every wind.

He must not go, she decided, or if he did, she would go with him. She prayed that she might be able to make him give up the project, and wrote strongly against it; but Augustine had already made up his mind. Then, in desperation, she set out for Carthage to make one last effort.

Her son was touched by her grief and her entreaties, but his plans were made: he was to start that very night. "I lied to my mother," he says, "and to such a mother!" He assured her that he was not going, that she might set her mind at rest. A friend of his was leaving Carthage, and he had promised to go down to the harbor to see him off.

Some instinct warned Monica that he was deceiving her. "I will go with you," she said. This was very awkward for her son, he was at his wit's end to know what to do. They went down to the harbor together, where they found Augustine's friend. No ship could put out that night, the sailors said, the wind was dead against them. The young men were unwilling to leave the harbor in case the wind should change and they should miss the boat, while Monica was determined not to leave Augustine.

They walked up and down together on the seashore in the cool evening air. The hours passed, and the situation became more and more difficult for Augustine. What was he to do? Monica was weary and worn out with grief. An idea suggested itself to him suddenly. It was no use waiting any longer, he said; it would be better to take some rest. The ship would certainly not start that night.

Monica was in no mood to rest, but Augustine knew her love of prayer. There was a little chapel on the seashore dedicated to St. Cyprian. Would she not at least go there and take shelter until the morning? He promised her again that he would not leave Carthage, and she at last consented, for her soul was full of sorrow.

Kneeling there in the stillness of the little chapel, she poured out the troubles of her heart to God, beseeching Him that He would not let Augustine leave her. The answer seemed a strange one. As she prayed, the wind suddenly changed; the sailors prepared to depart. Augustine and his friend went on board, and the ship set sail for Rome.

The last thing they saw as the shore faded away in the dim grey of the morning was the little chapel of St. Cyprian lying like a speck in the distance. But they did not see a lonely figure that stood on the sand and stretched out piteous hands to Heaven, wailing for the son whom she had lost a second time.

It was God alone who knew all the bitterness of that mother's heart. It was God alone who knew how, after the first uncontrollable outburst of grief, she bent herself in faith and love to endure the heartbreak—silent and uncomplaining. And it was only God who knew that the parting that seemed so cruel was to lead to the granting of her lifelong prayer, was to be the first stage in her son's conversion.

"She turned herself to Thee to pray for me," says Augustine, "and went about her accustomed affairs, and I arrived at Rome."

It seemed, indeed, as if his arrival in Rome was destined to be the end of his earthly career, for soon afterward he was attacked by a violent fever and lay at death's door. He was lodging in the house of a Manichaean, for, although he no longer held with their doctrines, he had many friends among them in Carthage who had recommended him to some of their sect in Rome.

Augustine himself was convinced that he owed his life at this time to his mother's prayers. God would not, for her sake, let him be cut off thus in all his sins, unbaptized and unrepentant, lest that mother's heart should be broken and her prayers unanswered. He recovered, and began to teach.

St. Augustine deceives his mother and sails away to Rome.

Already while he was in Carthage, Augustine had suspected that the lives of the Manichaeans were not much better than those of the heathens among whom they lived, although they gave out that their creed was the only one likely to reform human nature. In Rome his suspicions were confirmed. Thinking that Augustine was altogether one of themselves, they threw off the mask and showed themselves in their true colors.

The pagans at least were honest. They professed openly that they lived for nothing but enjoyment; and in this great city, even more than in Carthage, one could learn how low a man might fall; but at least they were not hypocrites. Augustine resolved to cut himself adrift from the Manichaeans altogether.

There was a Christian Rome within the pagan Rome, but of this Augustine knew nothing. On the throne of the Fisherman sat St. Damasus, wise and holy. His secretary, St. Jerome, was already famous, no less for his eloquence than for the greatness of his character. Jerome, like Augustine, had been carried away in his youth by the downward tide, but had returned to God by a glorious penance. The descendants of the oldest Roman families were to be found in the hospitals tending the sick or working among the poor in the great city. The first monasteries were growing up, little centers of faith and prayer in the desert. They were peopled by men and women who had counted the world well lost for Christ, or by those who to save their souls had fled, as the great St. Benedict was to do later, from the corruptions that had dragged down so many into the abyss.

Augustine had been greatly attracted shortly before leaving Carthage by the preaching of Helpidius, a Catholic priest. The idea came to him while in Rome to go to the Catholics and find out what they really taught. But he dismissed it. The Manichaeans had already told him, he reflected, that no intelligent man could accept their doctrines. Besides, they were too strict, their ideals were too high, he would have to give up too much.

One more honest impulse was stifled. Augustine entered a school of philosophers who professed to believe in nothing. It was, he decided, the wisest philosophy he knew.

Chapter 9

AUGUSTINE'S GREAT STRUGGLE COMES TO A HEAD

AUGUSTINE had not been a year in Rome before he discovered that the ways of the Roman students were not quite so delightful as he had been led to believe. They were less insolent, it is true, than those of Carthage, and not so rough; but they had other defects which were quite as trying. They would, for instance, attend the classes of a certain professor until the time arrived to pay their fees, when, deserting in a body to another school, they would proceed to play the same trick there. It was certainly one way of getting an education for nothing, but it was hard on the teachers. It seemed scarcely the profession in which one would be likely to make a fortune, even if it were possible to earn one's daily bread. Augustine was discouraged and sick at heart; everything seemed to be against him; there was no hope, no light anywhere. His life seemed doomed to be a failure, in spite of all his gifts.

And then, quite suddenly, came the opening that he had longed for. Symmachus, the Prefect of Rome, received a letter from Milan requesting him to name a professor of rhetoric for the vacant chair in that city. A competition was announced in which Symmachus, himself a well-known orator, was to be the judge. Augustine entered and won the prize. It was an excellent and honorable position. The professor was supported by the State. The Emperor Valentinian held his court in the city, which gave it a certain position.

Augustine was furnished with letters of introduction to Ambrose, the Bishop, who had been brilliantly successful at the bar in his youth and was probably an old friend of Symmachus. He was of a noble Roman family and famous alike for his great learning and peculiar charm of manner. He was famous also for his holiness of life, but this was of less interest to Augustine; it was Ambrose the orator with whom he desired to make acquaintance.

No sooner had he arrived in Milan than he presented himself before the Bishop, who received him with a cordial courtesy that attracted Augustine at once. The only way to judge of his eloquence was to attend the sermons at the cathedral. This Augustine began to do regularly. He found that Ambrose had not been over-praised. Augustine listened to him at first with the pleasure it always gave him to hear an eloquent speaker; then, gradually, with a shock of surprise, he began to attend to what the Bishop said as well as to his manner of saying it.

Ambrose was explaining the doctrines of the Church. He spoke very clearly and simply, to the intelligence no less than to the heart, for there were many catechumens in his congregation, as well as pagans who were seeking for the truth.

The Manichaeans had deceived him, then, thought Augustine. They had lied about the Church's teaching; or they themselves had been ignorant of it, and he had let himself be deceived. This was altogether unlike what they had told him. It was noble and sublime; all that was great and good in Augustine responded. Had he found the Truth at last?

In the meantime, Monica, determined to rejoin her son, arrived in Milan. The journey had been long and dangerous; they had been assailed by terrible storms, and even the sailors had lost courage. It was she who had comforted them in their fear. "The storm will soon be over," she assured them; "I know that we shall reach our journey's end in safety." Monica had a strong conviction that she would not die until her prayers had won Augustine back to God. The sailors took heart again at her words. Her calm eyes strengthened them; they felt that this gentle woman knew things that were hidden from them.

Monica's first visit was to St. Ambrose. The two noble natures understood each other at once. "Thank God for having given you such a mother," said the Bishop to Augustine, when he met him a few days later; "she is one in a thousand."

Much had happened since mother and son parted, and much had to be told. The first thing that Monica heard was that Augustine had left the Manichaeans. At this she rejoiced greatly; she was convinced, she told him, that she would see him a Catholic before she died. "Thus she spoke to me," says Augustine, "but to Thee, O Fountain of Mercy, she redoubled her prayers and her tears, beseeching Thee to hasten Thine aid and dispel my darkness."

They went together now to the sermons and sat side by side in the church, as in the days of Augustine's childhood. One by one he laid aside the false ideas of the truth that had been given to him by the Manichaeans. Everything was growing clearer to him every day. True, there was much that was above his understanding—above the understanding of any human being, as Ambrose frankly acknowledged—but not above their faith. The Manichaeans had sneered at faith as childish and credulous; and yet, thought Augustine, how many things he believed that he could have no possibility of proving. He believed, for instance, that Hannibal had crossed the Alps, although he had not been present at the time. He believed that Athens existed, although he had never been there. And if there was no foolishness in accepting these things on the testimony of men, why not accept others on the testimony of God?

As of old, a little group of friends had gathered round Augustine at Milan. There was Alypius, the most beloved of all his associates, who had taken the place of the dear, dead friend of his boyhood. There was Romanianus, who was there on State business, and Licentius, his son, with Trigetius, both pupils of Augustine's; Nebridius, who had been with him in Carthage and was, like himself, a native of Roman Africa; and several new friends he had made in Milan. It was agreed among them that they should set apart a certain time every day to seek for the truth, reading and discussing among themselves. The Scriptures were to form part of the reading.

"Great hope has dawned," wrote Augustine; "the Catholic Faith teaches not what we thought and vainly accused it of. Life is vain, [the time of] death uncertain; if it steals upon us of a sudden, in what state shall we depart hence? And where shall we learn what here we have neglected? Let us not delay to seek after God and the blessed life."

There was in Milan a holy old priest called Simplicianus, greatly beloved by St. Ambrose, for he had been his teacher and guide in early life. To him Augustine resolved to go; he might be able to help him. He told Simplicianus, among other things, that he had been reading a book of philosophy translated by a Roman called Victorinus. The book was good, said Simplicianus, but the story of Victorinus' own life was better. He had known him well in Rome. Augustine was interested; he would like to hear the story, he said.

Victorinus, said the old man, had been a pagan and a worshipper of the heathen gods. He was a famous orator and taught rhetoric to some of the noblest citizens of Rome. He was learned in every science and was so celebrated for his virtue that a statue had been erected to him in the forum. In his old age, after earnest study, he became a Christian, but remained a long time a catechumen through fears of what his friends would say. At last taking courage, he prepared himself for Baptism and, to punish himself for his human respect, insisted on reading his profession of faith aloud before the whole congregation instead of making it, as was usual, in private.

This courageous action of an old man made Augustine feel his own cowardice. He believed now that the Catholic Church was the true Church, and yet he could not face the thought of Baptism. He would have to give up so much. The Christian standard was high for a man who had spent his life in self-indulgence. He could never attain to it. He took leave of Simplicianus sadly; the help which he needed was not to be found there.

"I went about my usual business," he says, "while my anxiety increased, as I daily sighed to Thee." He frequented the church now even when there were no sermons, for he began to feel the need of prayer.

One day when Alypius and he were alone together, there came in a friend of theirs, Pontitianus, a devout Christian, who held a post at the Emperor's court. Finding the Epistles of St. Paul upon the table, he smiled at Augustine, saying that he was glad that he was reading them, for they were full of teaching. Pontitianus began to tell them about St. Antony of the Desert and of the many hermitages and monasteries in Egypt, and even here in his own country. He spoke to them of the monastic life and its virtues, and, seeing their interest and astonishment, went on to tell them of an incident that had happened a short time before.

Two young men of the Imperial Court, friends of his own, walking together in the country, came to a cottage inhabited by some holy recluses. A life of St. Antony lay on the table. One of the young men took it up and began to read. His first feeling was one of astonishment, his second of admiration. "How uncertain life is!" he said suddenly to his companion. "We are in the Emperor's service. I wish we were in God's; I would rather be His friend than the Emperor's." He read on, with sighs and groans. At last he shut the book and arose. "My mind is made up," he said, "I shall enter God's service here and now. If you will not do so too, at least do not try to hinder me."

"You have chosen well," said the other; "I am with you in this." They never left the hermitage.

This story only increased Augustine's misery. He had received more graces than these young men, and had wasted them; he was a coward. When Pontitianus had gone away, he left Alypius and went out into the garden. Alypius followed and sat down beside him.

"What are we about!" cried Augustine hotly. "The unlearned take Heaven by force, and we, with all our heartless learning, wallow in the mire!" He sank his face in his hands and groaned.

The way lay clear before him; he had found the Eternal Truth for which he had been seeking so long, and he had not the courage to go further.

This and that he would have to do; this and that he would have to give up—he could not: it was too hard.

And yet—to stand with both feet on the rock of truth, was it not worth all this and more?

So the battle raged. Good and evil struggled together in his soul.

It seemed to him then that he saw a long procession winding across the garden. It passed him and faded into the distance. First came boys and girls, young and weak, scarcely more than children, and they mocked him gently. "We have fought and conquered," they said, "even we." After them came a great multitude of men and women in the prime of life, some strong and vigorous, some feeble and sickly. It seemed to Augustine as if they looked at him with eyes full of contempt. "We have lived purely," they said, "we have striven and conquered." These were followed by old men and women, worn with age and suffering. They looked at him reproachfully. "We have fought and conquered," they said, "we have endured unto the end."

Augustine's self-control was leaving him; even Alypius' presence was more than he could bear. He leapt to his feet, went to the other end of the garden and, throwing himself down on the ground, wept as if his heart would break. His soul, tossed this way and that in its anguish, cried desperately to God for help.

Suddenly on the stillness of the summer afternoon, there broke the sound of a child's voice, sweet, insistent. "*Tolle, lege,*" it sang; "*tolle, lege*" ("Take and read"). Augustine stood up. There was no one there; no human being was in sight. "*Tolle, lege; tolle, lege,*" rang the sweet voice again and again in his ear, now on this side, now on that. Was this the answer to his prayer?

He remembered how St. Antony had opened the Sacred Scriptures on a like occasion and had found the help that he required. Going back to Alypius, he took up the sacred volume and opened it. "But put ye on the Lord Jesus Christ, and make not provision for the flesh in its concupiscences," he read.

Light, strength and conviction flowed into Augustine's soul. With God's help all things were possible; he would give up all and follow Him.

Then, having carefully marked the place, he sat down beside Alypius and told him of his resolution.

"What about me?" asked Alypius. "Perhaps there is something there for me too. Let me see." He took the book from Augustine, opened at the place he had marked, and read: "Now him that is weak in faith, take unto you."

"That will do very well for me," he said.

Augustine's first thought was for Monica. He must go to her, and at once. They sat together hand in hand until the sun sank in a rose-colored glory and the cool shadows of the evening fell like a blessing on the earth. There are some joys too deep for speech, too holy to be touched by mortal hands.

Chapter 10

MONICA'S PRAYERS ANSWERED

AMONG the Saints there are two great penitents, St. Mary Magdalen and St. Augustine, who in the first moment of their conversion shook themselves wholly free from the trammels of the past and never looked back again.

"Thou hast broken my bonds asunder!" cries St. Augustine; "to Thee will I offer the sacrifice of praise." Honors, wealth, pleasure, all the things he had desired so passionately were now as nothing to him. "For Thou didst expel them from me," he says, "and didst come in Thyself instead of them. And I sang to Thee, my Lord God, my true honor, my riches and my salvation."

The vacation time was close at hand. Augustine resolved to give up his professorship and to go away quietly to prepare himself for Baptism. Verecundus, one of the little group of faithful friends who surrounded him, had a country house in Cassiacum which he offered for Augustine's use while he remained in Italy.

It was a happy party that gathered within its walls. There were Augustine and his younger brother Navigius; the faithful Alypius, who was to receive Baptism with his friend; Licentius and Trigetius, Augustine's two pupils; and several others. Lastly there was Monica, who was a mother to them all and whose sunny presence did much to enliven the household. It was autumn, an Italian mid-September. The country was a glory of green and gold and crimson, the Apennines lying like purple shadows in the distance.

Here, in the seclusion that was so dear to his heart, Augustine read the Psalms for the first time. His soul was on fire with their beauty; every word carried him to God. Monica read with him, and he tells us that he would often turn to her for an explanation. "For," he continues, "she was walking steadily in the path in which I was as yet feeling my way."

There were other studies, besides, to be carried on, and St. Augustine tells us of some of the interesting discussions that were held on the lawn, or in the hall of the baths, which they used when the weather was not fine enough to go out.

One morning, when Augustine and his pupils were talking of the wonderful harmony and order that exist in nature, the door opened and Monica looked in.

"How are you getting on?" she asked, for she knew what they were discussing. Augustine invited her to join them, but Monica smiled. "I have never heard of a woman among the philosophers," she said.

"That is a mistake," replied Augustine. "There were women philosophers among the ancients, and you know, my dear mother, that I like your philosophy very much. Philosophy means nothing else but love of wisdom. Now you love wisdom even more than you love me, and I know how much that is. Why, you are so far advanced in wisdom that you fear no ill-fortune, not even death itself. Everybody says that this is the very height of philosophy. I will therefore sit at your feet as your disciple."

Monica, still smiling, told her son that he had never told so many lies in his life. In spite of her protests, however, they would not let her go, and she was enrolled among the philosophers. The discussions, says St. Augustine, owed a good deal of their beauty to her presence.

The 15th of November was Augustine's birthday. After dinner he invited his friends to come to the hall of the baths, that their souls might be fed also.

"For I suppose you all admit," he said, when they had settled themselves for conversation, "that we are made up of soul and body." To this everybody agreed but Navigius, who was inclined to argue and who said he did not know.

"Do you mean," asked Augustine, "that there is nothing at all that you do know, or that of the few things you do not know this is one?"

Navigius was a little put out at this question, but they pacified him and finally persuaded him to say that he was as certain of the fact that he was made up of body and soul as anybody could be. They then agreed that food was taken for the sake of the body.

"Must not the soul have its food too?" asked Augustine. "And what is that food? Is it not knowledge?"

Monica agreed to this, but Trigetius objected.

"Why, you yourself," said Monica, "are a living proof of it. Did you not tell us at dinner that you did not know what you were eating because you were lost in thought? Yet your teeth were working all the time. Where was your soul at that moment if not feeding too?"

Then Augustine, reminding them that it was his birthday, said that as he had already given them a little feast for the body, he would now give them one for the soul.

Were they hungry? he asked.

There was an eager chorus of assent.

"Can a man be happy," he asked, "if he has not what he wants, and is he happy if he has it?"

Monica was the first to answer this question. "If he wants what is good and has it," she replied, "he is happy. But if he wants what is bad, he is not happy even if he has it."

"Well said, Mother!" cried Augustine. "You have reached the heights of philosophy at a single bound."

Someone then said that if a man were needy, he could not be happy. Finally they all agreed that only he who possessed God could be wholly happy. But the discussion had gone on for a long time, and Augustine suggested that the soul as well as the body might have too much nourishment, and that it would be better to put off the rest until tomorrow.

The discussion was continued next day.

"Since only he who possesses God can be happy, who is he who possesses God?" asked Augustine, and they were all invited to give their opinion.

"He who leads a good life," answered one. "He who does God's will," said another. "He who is pure of heart," said a third. Navigius would not say anything, but agreed with the last speaker. Monica approved of them all.

St. Augustine continued: "It is God's will that all should seek Him?"

"Of course," they all replied.

"Can he who seeks God be leading a bad life?"

"Certainly not," they said.

"Can a man who is not pure in heart seek God?"

"No," they agreed.

"Then," said Augustine, "what have we here? A man who leads a good life, does God's will and is pure of heart, is seeking God. But he does not yet possess Him. Therefore we cannot uphold that they who lead good lives, do God's will, and are pure of heart, possess God."

They all laughed at the trap in which he had caught them. But Monica, saying that she was slow to grasp these things, asked to have the argument repeated. Then she thought a moment.

"No one can possess God without seeking Him," she said.

"True," said Augustine, "but while he is seeking he does not yet possess."

"I think there is no one who does not have God," she said. "But those who live well have Him for their friend, and those who live badly make themselves His enemies. Let us change the statement, 'He who possesses God is happy,' to 'He who has God for his friend is happy.'"

All agreed to this but Navigius.

"No," he said, "for this reason. If he is happy who has God for his friend (and God is the friend of those who seek Him, and those who seek Him do not possess Him, for to this all have agreed), then it is obvious that those who are seeking God have not what they want. And we all agreed yesterday that a man cannot be happy unless he has what he wants."

Monica could not see her way out of this difficulty, although she was sure there was one. "I yield," she said, "for logic is against me."

"Well," said Augustine, "we have reached the conclusion that he who has found God has Him for his friend and is happy; but he who is still seeking God has Him for his friend but is not yet happy. He, however, who has separated himself from God by sin has neither God for his friend nor is he happy."

This satisfied everybody.

The other side of the question was then considered.

"In what does unhappiness consist?" asked Augustine.

Monica maintained that neediness and unhappiness must go together. "For he who has not what he wants," she said, "is both needy and unhappy."

Augustine then supposed a man who had everything he wanted in this world. Could it be said that he was needy? Yet was it certain that he was happy?

Licentius suggested that there would remain with him the fear of losing what he had.

"That fear," replied Augustine, "would make him unhappy, but would not make him needy. Therefore we could have a man who is unhappy without being needy."

To this everyone agreed but Monica, who still argued that unhappiness could not be separated from neediness.

"This supposed man of yours," she said, "rich and fortunate, still fears to lose his good fortune. That shows that he wants [lacks] wisdom. Can we call a man who wants money needy and not call him so when he wants wisdom?"

At this remark there was a general outcry of admiration. It was the very argument, said Augustine, that he had meant to use himself.

"Nothing," said Licentius, "could have been more truly and divinely said. What, indeed, is more wretched than to lack wisdom? And the wise man can never be needy, whatever else he lacks."

Augustine then went on to define wisdom. "The wisdom that makes us happy," he said, "is the wisdom of God, and the wisdom of God is the Son of God. Perfect life is the only happy life," he continued, "and to this, by means of firm faith, cheerful hope and burning love we shall surely be brought if we but hasten toward it."

So the discussion ended, and all were content.

"Oh," cried Trigetius, "how I wish you would provide us with a feast like this every day!"

"Moderation in all things," answered Augustine. "If this has been a pleasure to you, it is God alone that you must thank." So the happy, innocent days flew past in the pursuit of that wisdom which is eternal.

"Too late have I loved Thee, O Beauty ever ancient, ever new!" cried Augustine. "Behold Thou wast within me, and I was abroad, and there I sought Thee. I have tasted Thee, and I am hungry after Thee. Thou hast touched me, and I am all on fire."

At the beginning of Lent (387 A.D.), Augustine and Alypius returned to Milan to attend the course of instructions which St. Ambrose was to give to those who were preparing for Baptism.

In the night between Holy Saturday and Easter Sunday, the stains of the past were washed away forever in those cleansing waters, and at the Mass of daybreak on that blessed morning Augustine knelt at the altar to receive the Lord. Monica was beside him; her tears and her prayers had been answered. She and her son were one again in heart and soul.

Chapter 11

THE DEATH OF A SAINT

IN the old days at Milan, before his conversion, Augustine had often told his friends that the dream of his life was to live quietly somewhere with a few friends who would devote themselves to the search for truth. It had even been proposed to try the scheme, but it would not work. Some of his friends were married, others had worldly ties that they could not break. The idea had to be given up.

Now he had found the Truth, and at Cassiacum his dream had been in a manner realized. Why should they not continue to live like that, he asked Alypius, at all events until they were ready for the work to which God had called them? And where should they live this life but in their own country, which was to be the future field of their labors?

Alypius asked nothing better. Their friend Evodius, like themselves a citizen of Tagaste, who had been baptized a short time before, was ready to join them. He held a high position at the court of the Emperor, but it seemed to him a nobler thing to serve the King of kings. So these three future bishops of the Church in Africa made their plans together. Monica would be the mother of the little household, as she had been at Cassiacum; she was ready to go wherever they wished.

A few days before they started an event occurred which they all remembered later. It was the feast of St. Cyprian, and Monica had returned from Mass absorbed in God, as she always was after Holy Communion. Perhaps she had been thinking of her night of anguish in the little chapel by the seashore at Carthage three years before, when God had seemed deaf to her prayers in order that He might grant her the fullness of her heart's desire.

Suddenly she turned to them with shining eyes.

"Let us hasten to Heaven!" she cried.

They gently questioned her as to what she meant, but she did not seem to hear them. "My soul and my flesh have rejoiced in the living God," she said, and they marvelled at the heavenly beauty of her face.

It was a long journey from Milan to Ostia on the Tiber, where they were to set sail for Africa. They remained there for some weeks, for the ship was not to start at once.

One evening Augustine and Monica were sitting together at a window that overlooked the garden and the sea. They were talking of Heaven, St. Augustine tells us, asking each other what that eternal life of the Saints must be which eye hath not seen nor ear heard. How small in comparison were the things of earth, they said, even the most beautiful of God's creations; for all these things were less than He who made them. As their two souls stretched out together towards the infinite Love and Wisdom, it seemed to them that for one moment, with one beat of the heart, they touched It, and the joy of that moment was a foreshadowing of eternity.

They sighed as it faded from them, and they were forced to return again to the things of earth.

"Son," said Monica, "there is nothing in this world now that gives me any delight. What have I to do here any longer? I know not, for all I desired is granted. There was only one thing for which I wished to live, and that was to see you a Christian and a Catholic before I died. And God has given me even more than I asked, for He has made you one of His servants, and you now desire no earthly happiness. What am I doing here?"

About five days afterward she fell ill of a fever. They thought she was tired with the long journey and would soon be better, but she grew

Ostia: "The joy of that moment
was like a foretaste of eternity."

worse and was soon unconscious. When she opened her eyes, Augustine and Navigius were watching by her bed.

"You will bury your mother here," she said. Augustine could not trust himself to speak; but Navigius, who knew how great had been her desire to be buried at Tagaste beside her husband, protested. "Oh, why are we not at home," he cried, "where you would wish to be!" Monica looked at him reproachfully. "Do you hear what he says?" she asked Augustine. "Bury my body anywhere," she said; "it does not matter. Do not let that disturb you. This only I ask—that you remember me at the altar of God wherever you may be."

To another person, who asked her if it would not be a sorrow to her to be buried in a land so far from home, Monica answered, "One is never far from God."

It was not only her sons who grieved, but the faithful friends who were with them, for was she not their mother too? Had she not taken as much care of them as if they had been her children?

Augustine scarcely left her side, and she was glad to have him with her. As she thanked him one day for some little thing he had done for her, his lip quivered. She thought he was thinking of all the suffering he had caused her, and smiled at him with tender eyes. "You have always been a good son to me," she said. "Never have I heard a harsh or reproachful word from your lips."

"My life was torn in two," says Augustine. "That life which was made up of mine and hers."

They were all with her when she passed peacefully away a few days later. They choked back their tears. "It did not seem meet," says Augustine, "to celebrate that death with groans and lamentations. Such things were fit for a less blessed deathbed, but not for hers."

Then, as they knelt gazing at the beloved face that seemed to be smiling at some unseen mystery, Evodius had a happy inspiration. Taking up the Psalter, he opened it at the 110th Psalm.

"I will praise Thee, O Lord, with my whole heart," he sang softly, "in the council of the just, and in the congregation."

"Great are the works of the Lord," sang the others with trembling voices, "sought out according to all His wills." Friends and religious women who had gathered near the house to pray entered and joined in the chant. It was the voice of rejoicing rather than the cry of grief that followed that pure soul on its way to Heaven. Augustine alone was silent, for his heart was breaking.

We are but human, after all, and the sense of their loss fell upon them all later. That night Augustine lay thinking of his mother's life and the unselfish love of which it had been so full. "Thy handmaid, so pious toward Thee, so careful and tender toward us. And I let go my tears," he tells us, "and let them flow as much as they would. I wept for her who for so many years had wept for me."

They buried her, as she herself had foretold, in Ostia, where her sacred relics were found a thousand years later by Pope Martin V and carried to the Church of St. Augustine in Rome.

The memory of the mother to whom he owed so much remained with Augustine until the day of his death. He loved to speak of her. Thirty years later, while preaching to his people at Hippo, he said:

"The dead do not come back to us. If it were so, how often should I see my holy mother at my side! She followed me over sea and land into far countries that she might not lose me forever. God forbid that she should be less loving now that she is more blessed. Ah, no! she would come to help and comfort me, for she loved me more than I can tell."

Monica was seen no more on this earth. But who that has followed the career of the great Bishop and Doctor of the Church can doubt that she who prayed for him so fervently on earth continued to pray for him in Heaven?

THE CONFRATERNITY OF CHRISTIAN MOTHERS

(Added by the Publisher, 1998.)

In the mid-nineteenth century in France, an Association of Christian Mothers was formed under the patronage of St. Monica. The members offered mutual prayers for children and husbands who had gone astray. The association was raised to the rank of an archconfraternity and grew rapidly, spreading to many countries.

In the United States, the Confraternity of Christian Mothers was canonically erected in 1881 in St. Augustine's Church, Pittsburgh, then was raised to the rank of an archconfraternity with the right of affiliating other confraternities whenever the Ordinary approved. Since then, over 3,400 confraternities have been affiliated with the Pittsburgh Archconfraternity, which is directed by the Capuchin Fathers and Brothers.

The Confraternity of Christian Mothers desires to sanctify wives and mothers by several means— by frequent and regular prayers in common with thousands of other women in the same vocation, by talks and discussions, by the frequentation of the Sacraments, and by the edifying example of the other members.

The object of the Confraternity of Christian Mothers is the Christian home education of children by truly Christian mothers, training and sanctifying the young ones entrusted to their care. Members are schooled to edify one another by word and deed, to support one another by fervent prayers and thus become the mainstay of spiritual life within their own family and a fruitful source of blessings to the community in which they live. The Pittsburgh Archconfraternity publishes a prayer book entitled *Mother Love*.

The U.S. address of the Archconfraternity of Christian Mothers is 220 37th St., Pittsburgh, PA 15201-9990.

Affiliated with the Archconfraternity is a movement or association called St. Monica's Circle. The purpose of St. Monica's Circle is to pray for "vocations in the parish." Information may be obtained from the above address.

PRAYERS
(Added by the Publisher, 1998.)

LITANY OF ST. MONICA
For private recitation only.

Lord, have mercy on us.
Christ, have mercy on us.
Lord, have mercy on us. Christ, hear us.
Christ, graciously hear us.
God the Father of Heaven, *have mercy on us.*
God, the Son, Redeemer of the world, *have mercy
    on us.*
God the Holy Spirit, *have mercy on us.*
Holy Trinity, one God, *have mercy on us.*

Holy Mary, conceived without stain of original
    sin, *pray for us and for our children.*
Holy Mary, glorious Mother of Jesus Christ, *pray
    for us and for our children.*
St. Monica, *etc.*
Model of wives,
You who converted your unbelieving husband,
Mother of St. Augustine,
Strict and prudent teacher, guardian of your son
    in all his ways,

You who carefully watched over his conduct,

You who were sorely distressed at his erring from the right,

You who were untiring in your petitions for his soul's safety,

You who still hoped on amid the bitterness of your heart and your floods of tears,

You who were filled with consolation upon his return to God,

You who died calmly after faithfully fulfilling your duties,

You who are the prayerful intercessor of all mothers who pray and weep as you did,

Preserve the innocence of our children, *we beseech you, St. Monica.*

Protect them against the deceits of evil men, *we beseech you, St. Monica.*

Protect them from the dangers of bad example, *etc.*

Protect them from the snares of the spirits of Hell,

Watch over the movements of grace in their hearts,

Let the Christian virtues strike deep root in their hearts and bear much fruit,

Redouble your intercession for youth approaching manhood,

Obtain for all in mortal sin true contrition and

perfect conversion,

Obtain for all mothers to fulfill their duties steadily and perseveringly,

Commend all mothers to the protection of the ever-blessed Virgin Mother of Our Lord,

Favorably incline the heart of your beloved son Augustine to the salvation of our children,

St. Augustine, holy son of a saintly mother, *pray for us and for our children.*

Lamb of God, Who takes away the sins of the world, *spare us, O Lord!*

Lamb of God, Who takes away the sins of the world, *graciously hear us, O Lord!*

Lamb of God, Who takes away the sins of the world, *have mercy on us, O Lord!*

V. Pray for us, O holy St. Monica,

R. That we may be made worthy of the promises of Christ.

Let us pray

O GOD, Who observed the devout tears and pleading of St. Monica and granted to her prayers the conversion of her husband and the penitential return of her son Augustine, grant us the grace to implore Thee also with earnest zeal, so that we may obtain, as she did, the salvation of our own soul and the souls of those belonging to us. Through Christ our Lord. Amen.

O holy Monica, by your patience and prayers you obtained from God the conversion of your husband and the grace to live in peace with him; obtain for us, we beseech you, the blessing of Almighty God, so that true harmony and peace may reign also in our homes, and that all the members of our families may attain eternal life. Amen.

O holy Monica, by your burning tears and unceasing prayers you saved your son from eternal damnation. Obtain for us the grace ever to comprehend what is most conducive to the salvation of our children, so that we may effectively restrain them from sin and lead them by virtue and piety to Heaven! Amen.

NOVENA PRAYER

FAITHFUL GOD, Light of all hearts, we praise Thee for Saint Monica, woman of living faith and reconciling love. She nursed her son, Augustine, on the Name of Jesus, and urged him tirelessly to a Christian way of life. In answer to her prayers for his conversion Thou gavest her greater joy than all her tears had dared to ask.

Hear our prayers: (*here mention your request*). As once Thou didst captivate the heart of St. Augustine, so now draw our hearts to Thee, O Beauty ever ancient, ever new.

MOTHER'S PRAYER FOR THE INTERCESSION OF ST. AUGUSTINE

O GOD, Who enlightened St. Augustine by Thy grace and inflamed him with Thy love amid the darkness and miseries of a life of sin, have mercy likewise on my poor soul and upon those of my children and relatives! Pardon our ingratitude, our disobedience, our want of reverence, our indifference, and all the offenses of which we have ever been guilty against Thy holy Name.

We acknowledge that there is in this world no pain or punishment so severe as that which we deserve; therefore, full of dread of what is in store for us, we invoke the intercession of Thy holy servant Augustine, so inflamed with love of Thee!

O holy penitent Augustine, seraph of divine love, unspeakable miracle of divine mercy, obtain for us from God a true, perfect and heartfelt sorrow for our sins, a devout and constant love of God, a love that triumphs over all difficulties, temptations and tribulations, and a wise and unremitting fervor in the observance of the divine Commandments and the fulfillment of our duties.

Assist us especially in the training of our dear children. Their virtue and innocence are exposed to many dangers in the world! See how numerous are the snares and deceits prepared for the ruin of their souls by the flesh, and through the words and example of evil and worldly-minded men. If they do not receive extraordinary help, how can they withstand such allurements?

O great St. Augustine, take them under your protection! To our efforts in their behalf, join your intercession for them with God. Exert all your influence and, with the compassion of your loving heart, intercede with the Most Holy Trinity for them. Permit not that our children, sanctified in the waters of Baptism, should through mortal sin be banished from the presence of God and suffer eternal punishment.

Preserve them from the greatest of all evils here below, namely, that of denying the love of Jesus Christ through affection to some creature or the fear of some misfortune. Rather let them, and us their parents, die in the grace of God than live to offend Him mortally. This favor we implore through your intercession, O holy son of a sainted mother, you who gladly receive and graciously hear the prayers of a mother. I confidently hope that you have already heard my petitions, and that you will obtain for me a favorable answer from God. Amen.

DAILY PRAYER FOR THE CHILDREN
Recited daily by members of the Confraternity of Christian Mothers

O MARY, Immaculate Virgin and Sorrowful Mother, commend our beloved children to the Most Sacred Heart of Jesus, who refuses nothing to His Mother.

Holy Guardian Angels, *pray for them.*
St. Joseph, powerful patron, *pray for them.*
St. John, beloved disciple of the Heart of Jesus, *pray for them.*
St. Augustine, *pray for them.*
St. Anthony, *pray for them.*
St. Aloysius, *pray for them.*
St. Anne, Mother of Our Lady, *pray for them.*
St. Elizabeth, *pray for them.*
St. Monica, *pray for them.* Amen.

If you have enjoyed this book, consider making your next selection from among the following . . .

ABOUT THE AUTHOR

This book was authored by Mother Frances Alice Monica Forbes, a sister of the Society of the Sacred Heart, Scotland.

The future author was born on March 16, 1869 and was named Alice Forbes. Alice's mother died when she was a child, and her father became the dominant influence in her life, helping to form Alice's virile personality and great capacity for work. She was raised as a Presbyterian.

In 1900 Alice became a Catholic. The Real Presence in the Eucharist had been the big stumbling-block to her conversion, but one day she was hit by the literal truth of Our Lord's words: "This is My Body." Only a few months after her conversion, she entered the Society of the Sacred Heart, becoming a 31-year-old postulant. She seems to have received her vocation at her First Communion, when Our Lord kindled in her heart "the flame of an only love."

In the convent, Sister Forbes used her keen intelligence and strong will to make generously and completely the sacrifices that Our Lord asked of her each day. She put great store by the virtue of obedience. Much of the latter part of her life was spent in illness and suffering, yet she was always kind and uncomplaining—a charming person and a "gallant" soul. Throughout her sufferings the most important thing to her was the love of God. She died in 1936.

Mother Frances Alice Monica Forbes wrote many

books, including a series of interesting short lives of selected Saints called "Standard Bearers of the Faith." One of these books, that on Pope St. Pius X, was very highly regarded by Cardinal Merry del Val, who was a close friend of Pope Pius X.

Other works by Mother Frances Alice Monica Forbes include *St. Ignatius Loyola, St. John Bosco: Friend of Youth, St. Teresa, St. Columba, St. Athanasius, St. Catherine of Siena, St. Benedict, St. Hugh of Lincoln, The Gripfast Series of English Readers* and *The Gripfast Series of History Readers*, various plays, and a number of other books.

The above information is from the book *Mother F. A. Forbes: Religious of the Sacred Heart—Letters and Short Memoir*, by G. L. Sheil (London: The Catholic Book Club, 1948, by arrangement with Longmans, Green & Co., Ltd.).